MEXICO CITY
THE CITY AT A GLANCE

D1321842

Avenida Presidente Masaryk
Mexico City's Fifth Avenue traverses Polanco, and is lined with some of the city's swankiest stores and showrooms. It is also the main drag for upscale nightclubs and restaurants.

Torre Pemex
Built in 1984, this 52-storey tower, owned by Mexican oil monopoly Pemex (Petróleos Mexicanos), dominates the city's skyline.
Marina Nacional 329, Huasteca

El Zócalo
The world's third largest square is located in the densely packed city centre. It was the site of the ancient Aztec city of Tenochtitlan and is now home to tourists and demonstrators.

Paseo de la Reforma
The city's main drag is to Mexico City what the Champs-Elysées is to Paris, and it has recently been given a Las Ramblas-style makeover, making it a pleasant place to go for an afternoon stroll.

Roma
Home to Mexico City's creative crowd, this fashionable, leafy, low-rise neighbourhood holds some of the city's most cutting-edge boutiques, bars and galleries, but it is also pleasantly lacking in pretension.

Chapultepec
A welcome green expanse, the park holds many of the city's attractions, from museums to boating lakes.

Torre Mayor
This is Mexico City's tallest building, which overlooks Chapultepec Park. It has 55 floors, with a public observatory on the 52nd.
Paseo de la Reforma 505

INTRODUCTION
THE CHANGING FACE OF THE URBAN SCENE

Something drastic has happened to Mexico City over the past decade. Stroll down the refurbished Paseo de la Reforma, which has become a leafy, boulevardier's delight, and you'll find more chauffeur-driven BMWs idling outside the boutiques of Avenida Presidente Masaryk than you'll find in Bel Air or on Bond Street. The Roma and Condesa neighbourhoods have established themselves as elegant staging posts for the city's gilded youth, while the exodus of the wealthy from the city centre to the heavily guarded suburbs has been partly arrested by the rebirth of San Ángel.

In short, Mexico City has transformed itself from a city that's renowned for its pollution and security problems, into the dashing and voguish capital of Latin America. It might be due to improved trading links with the US, or the end of the 71-year rule of the Institutional Revolutionary Party (PRI) in 2000. Perhaps it was the introduction of democracy in 1997, when *Chilangos* (Mexico City residents) were first able to elect their own mayor. Or it's the 'zero tolerance' policy on security that former New York mayor, Rudolph Giuliani, helped the city devise. Certainly, the decision to force industry outside the city in 1989, and the introduction of the *hoy no circula* ('don't drive today') policy, to reduce the number of cars on the streets, have been major factors: pollution levels have plummeted. Whatever the causes, Mexico City (DF, Distrito Federal, as it's called locally), has spruced up its act. It's never been so sexy.

ESSENTIAL INFO
FACTS, FIGURES AND USEFUL ADDRESSES

TOURIST OFFICE
Nuevo León 56
T 5553 1901
www.visitmexico.com

TRANSPORT
Car hire
Avis, *T 5762 3262*
Hertz, *T 5571 3262*
Taxis
Sitio 300, T 5571 9344
Metro
T 5709 1133

EMERGENCY SERVICES
Ambulance
T 080
Police
T 066
Tourist Police
T 5552 1569/5522 3805
24-hour pharmacy
República del Salvador 81, 85 and 97
El Centro
T 5709 5349/5709 3211

CONSULATES
British Embassy
Río Lerma 71
Cuauhtémoc
T 45242 8500
American Embassy
Paseo de la Reforma 305
Cuauhtémoc
T 5080 2000

MONEY
American Express
Camino Real, Mariano Escobedo 700
Polanco
T 5263 8888
www10.americanexpress.com

POSTAL SERVICES
Post Office
Tacuba 1/Eje Central
Lázaro Cárdenas
T 5512 0091
Shipping
Abromex
T 5584 2025
www.abromex.com

BOOKS
The Mexico City Reader
edited by Ruben Gallo
(University of Wisconsin Press)
The Most Transparent Region
by Carlos Fuentes (Alfaguara)
The Plumed Serpent by DH Lawrence
(Cambridge University Press)

WEBSITES
Art
www.lacoleccionjumex.com
www.artemexicano.com/eguerrero
www.kurimanzutto.com
www.barragan-foundation.com
Newspapers
www.reforma.com
www.economista.com.mx

COST OF LIVING
Taxi from Benito Juárez
International Airport
to El Centro
€10
Coffee
€1.80
Packet of cigarettes
€1.50
Daily newspaper
€0.55
Bottle of champagne
€121

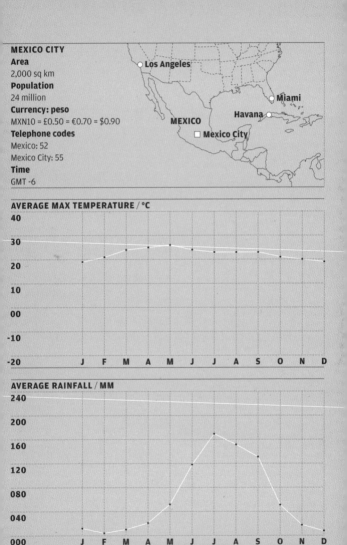

MEXICO CITY
Area
2,000 sq km
Population
24 million
Currency: peso
MXN10 = £0.50 = €0.70 = $0.90
Telephone codes
Mexico: 52
Mexico City: 55
Time
GMT -6

Los Angeles

Miami

Havana

MEXICO

☐ Mexico City

AVERAGE MAX TEMPERATURE / °C

40												
30												
20												
10												
00												
-10												
-20	J	F	M	A	M	J	J	A	S	O	N	D

AVERAGE RAINFALL / MM

240												
200												
160												
120												
080												
040												
000	J	F	M	A	M	J	J	A	S	O	N	D

NEIGHBOURHOODS

THE AREAS YOU NEED TO KNOW AND WHY

To help you navigate the city, we've chosen the most interesting districts (see the map inside the back cover) and underlined featured venues in colour, according to their location (see below); those venues that are outside these areas are not coloured.

CONDESA

A fashionable district, full of chic bars and cantinas, and tree-lined avenues, once inhabited by European immigrants and an industrious middle class. Art deco in design, it was built around the former race track, which can still be seen in the shape of Parque México. In 1985, it was almost destroyed in an earthquake; today, the damage has been repaired and any holes plugged with aluminium-and-glass loft spaces by sought-after architectural firms.

EL CENTRO

Once the centre of social and economic life, this is where Spanish conquerors founded a city on the site of México-Tenochtitlan, the Aztec citadel. In the 20th century, the elite deserted their palaces here for the suburbs and the area began to decline. In the 1950s, when the National University moved to Ciudad Universitaria (see p057), its fate was sealed. Today, Fundación del Centro Historico is working, together with the government, to improve the area.

ROMA

Home to a creative crowd and some of the city's best galleries, boutiques and cafés. The *fin-de-siècle* architecture reflects the aspirations of an aristocracy longing to live up to European standards. Ornate apartment blocks and stylish villas abound, but what gives Roma its stylish edge is the coexistence of varied architectonic styles, social classes and nationalities.

POLANCO

This district is the last remaining urban neighbourhood to offer a home to the wealthy (the few who haven't relocated to the suburbs). It's Upper East Side meets Beverly Hills, with expensive restaurants, boutiques and hotels, and broad, palm-lined boulevards. Avenida Presidente Masaryk is the city's Fifth Avenue and is frequently packed with chauffeur-driven BMWs hovering outside Fendi, Louis Vuitton, Gucci and Hermès.

ALAMEDA

Surrounding the 16th-century park of the same name, this district houses some of the most important landmarks, from Torre Latinoamericana (see p060) to Museo del Palacío de Bellas Artes (T 5512 1410), the ornate Palacio Postal (see p062) and Museo Mural Diego Rivera (T 5512 0754).

CHAPULTEPEC

This district is the overworked lungs of Mexico City, a vast swathe of green on the map. Sitting between some of the city's main arteries, it is bordered by its most important districts. Pleasantly leafy and undulating, it's home to many extra-curricular attractions of the city: boating lakes and playing fields, Parque Zoológico (T 5553 6229) and many museums, including the brilliant Museo Nacional de Antropología (see p014) and Mexican artist Rufino Tamayo's Museo Tamayo Arte Contemporáneo (T 5286 6519).

LANDMARKS
THE SHAPE OF THE CITY SKYLINE

Getting to grips with Mexico City's geography is not easy, due to its size (it's one of the world's largest cities). The mountains that surround it are no help to navigation, as they can't be seen from most of its streets, and the sights are spread liberally around the sprawl. On the other hand, there's no mistaking where you are; the city is visually distinctive, from the purple jacaranda trees in spring and the omnipresent green Beetle taxis, to the murals and Aztec incidentals on buildings and monuments, and the mix of colonial edifices and minimalist glass and stainless steel.

El Centro offers the most landmarks, from El Zócalo, the expansive square at its heart, edged by <u>Catédral Metropolitana</u> and the <u>Palacio Nacional</u> (Avenida Pino Suarez), to <u>Palacio Postal</u> (see p062), with the city's first skyscraper nearby in Alameda: <u>Torre Latinoamericano</u> (see p060). From here, if you follow Paseo de la Reforma south, you can take in a monument at every major crossroads, including El Ángel de la Independencia (at the junction with Rio Tiber). Carry on south and you'll reach Chapultepec, a vast urban garden, peppered with lakes, and museums, most notably <u>Museo Nacional de Antropología</u> (see p014). Others are far flung, from Agustín Hernández's spaceship (see p011), to the architectural wonders of Ciudad Universitaria (see p057) in the south, and Basílica de Guadalupe (see p013) in the north.

For all addresses, see Resources.

Agustín Hernández's Home/Office
This innovative building was built 35 years ago, on the vertiginously steep, wooded slopes of Bosques de las Lomas. It's the work of local architect Agustín Hernández and serves as his home and office. The area alone is worth a visit, as it is full of remarkable residences, many by Hernández or his acolytes, and you get great views back over the city.
Bosque Acacias, T 5596 1554

Torres de Satélite

These five, colourful, reinforced-concrete towers, 30-50m high, rise dramatically, from the central reservation of Periférico, Mexico City's main ring road. Designed in the late 1950s by architect Luis Barragán and sculptor Mathias Goeritz, these urban sculptures mark the end of the city and the beginning of Ciudad Satélite (Satellite City). The area was conceived as a self-contained urban utopia for the middle classes, but it's now an indistinguishable part of the urban sprawl. Barragán and Goeritz subsequently argued for the popular monuments, which sadly cost them their friendship, ending a fruitful collaboration that had lasted for 20 years. To take in the monumental scale of the towers, stop in the nearby parking bay and walk between them.

Periférico Norte, Ciudad Satélite

Basílica de Guadalupe

This modern basilica, a massive teepee construction built in the mid-1970s by Pedro Ramírez Vásquez, dominates the hillside area north of the city known as La Villa. Alongside is the 16th-century church on the spot where, on 12 December 1531, it is said that the Virgin of Guadalupe appeared to Juan Diego Cuauhlatoatzin. In 2002, Pope John Paul II made Juan Diego a saint and every year, on 12 December, millions of Guadalupe residents make a pilgrimage to the basilica from the villages. Inside, a moving walkway takes visitors past a shrine to the Virgin.

Plaza de las Américas 1, Villa de Guadalupe

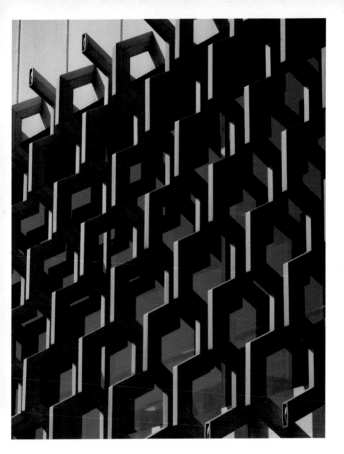

Museo Nacional de Antropología

If you have time to visit only one museum, this should be it. Opened in 1964 and designed by the architect Pedro Ramírez Vásques, this is the jewel in the crown of Chapultepec. The low-rise building is a vast, 44,000 sq m structure of white marble. A solid canopy covers much of the central patio (left), which is held up by a large carved-bronze column, down which water cascades. This fascinating museum takes visitors through the history of Mexico, before the arrival of the Spanish. There are many fascinating exhibits here, including the Aztec Calendar Stone, a stone carved with an early pre-Columbian calendar, reconstructions of the pyramid of the Aztec ruler Quetzalcóatl, and a replica of a tomb from the ancient Maya. *Paseo de la Reforma, T 5553 6253, www.mna.inah.gob.mx*

HOTELS

WHERE TO STAY AND WHICH ROOMS TO BOOK

Once, a trip to Mexico City was typically brought on by a business fixture, or was simply a stopover, en route to the beach or temples. This meant spending a night or two in one of the city's anonymous 1970s hotel chains. Happily, things have changed, thanks to the Micha brothers and Carlos Couturier, who opened the minimalist Habita (see p026) in Polanco in 2000, transforming the city's hospitality offering. Three years later, W Mexico City (see p024) arrived, the W hotel chain's first in Latin America. Then, in 2005, the Micha brothers and Couturier opened a second boutique hotel, Condesa DF (see p020), inspired by its fashionable location. So the city is now a destination for the high-end tourist.

Many of the older hotels have now undergone sophisticated redesigns and added services, such as Polanco's Intercontinental Presidente (see p030). Indeed, if there's anything at all to lament in Mexico City's resurgent hotel scene, it's the quality of some of these refurbishment programmes. Sadly, the formerly fabulous Camino Real (see p028) has seen much of its original decor ousted. There are, we will concede, one or two hotels that have remained gloriously unchanged. Those of you who are after a taste of old-school Mexico should investigate the Majestic (Francisco I Madero 73, T 5521 8600) and the fabulous Gran Hotel (see opposite), converted from a former department store.
For all addresses and room rates, see Resources.

Gran Hotel

This grand building started life, at the turn of the century, as a spectacular department store, but its stately interior was easily converted into a hotel in later years. The stunning art nouveau lobby (above) is covered by a beautiful, vast stained-glass canopy. Filigree railings edge the balconied upper floors and brass-cage lifts take guests to and from their rooms. To underscore the aura of grandeur, elaborate chandeliers dangle and birds sing from cages. The rooms are also decorated in the art-nouveau style, but, otherwise, the facilities are very 21st century and cater for the business crowd. Take a seat at the café on the terrace, where you'll get wonderful views of El Zócalo and the buildings that surround it. *Avenida 16 de Septiembre 82, T 1083 7700, www.granhotelciudaddemexico.com.mx*

Master Suite, Gran Hotel

Condesa DF

Located in Avenida Veracruz, a street lined with purple Jacaranda trees, in a converted 1928 apartment building, Condesa DF's classical facade harks back to the neighbourhood's belle époque. Hip local architects Higuera & Sánchez, have refurbished the interior structure to offer a modern patio clad with vertical white shutters (right), and Paris-based designer India Mahdavi has introduced a sensual atmosphere to the interiors: blue walls, tropical plants, low wicker chairs and marble tables. The restaurant serves modern basics like tequila black cod. The bar has its own signature mezcal, served in bottles designed for the hotel. With a cinema and a dance club in the basement you can see why the Balcony Suite (above) or, even better, the Top Suite (overleaf) are our favourite places to stay.
Avenida Veracruz 102, T 5241 2600
www.condesadf.com

W Mexico City

Located in upscale Polanco, the W's first hotel in Latin America combines the chain's slick styling with Mexican sensuality. If the 280 sq m Presidential Suite, with its James Bond decor, is booked, console yourself with the Cool Corner Suite (right), which has a superb tub and pressure shower, and is stocked with Bliss bathroom products. W's lobby bar, the Living Room, starts buzzing from 6pm with thirtysomething bachelors and pinstriped businessmen supping cocktails. Upstairs, you'll find Solea, W's restaurant, which combines Asian and Mexican influences in dishes such as grilled scallops with *achiote*, red snapper with chorizo, and hot chocolate cake with ancho chilli. All your needs are taken care of with W's 'whatever, whenever' service.

Campos Elíseos 252, T 9138 1800, www.starwoodhotels.com/whotels

Habita
One of our favoured hotels in the city, it has 36 rooms inside an etched-glass box designed by TEN architects. Enjoy a swim in the rooftop pool (below) and have a sauna in the spa by day; by night, the city's elite gather on the nearby bar and terrace as arthouse movies are projected onto the building next door.
Avenida Presidente Masaryk 201, T 5282 3100, www.hotelhabita.com

Camino Real
Built for the 1968 Olympics by Mexican architect Ricardo Legorreta, the Camino Real's architecture was inspired by the teachings of Luis Barragán, and captures perfectly the colourful start he gave to Mexican modernism. Recently refurbished, after a change of ownership, it has, sadly, lost the huge Alexander Calder sculpture, pink Florence Knoll sofas, purple wool carpets and lamps with glass spheres as bases, which used to be in the lobby. What does remain is Rufino Tamayo's mural, Mathias Goeritz's golden wall and his pink screen at the entrance, as well as the fountain in the forecourt. If you're staying here, Wallpaper* recommends booking the Presidential Suite (above) and having a drink in the new floating Blue Lounge (see p041), but not without a certain nostalgia for what was lost.
Mariano Escobedo 700, T 5263 8888, www.caminoreal.com/mexico

Intercontinental Presidente
In stark contrast to the intimacy of the newer hotels, this 42-floor, 659-room monolith, built in the 1970s, has more style than most, thanks to smart wooden floors, a stunning lobby (below) and a piano bar. It's popular with the business community, but its restaurant, Au Pied de Cochon, is bringing in a fresh crowd. *Campos Eliseos 218, T 5327 7700, www.ichotelsgroup.com*

24 HOURS

SEE THE BEST OF THE CITY IN JUST ONE DAY

Sadly, for visitors with an environmental conscience, the only way to get the most from 24 hours in this sprawling city is to fly in the face of the *hoy no circula* ('don't drive today') spirit and go by car. Mexico City has a rich arts heritage and a distinctive take on modernist architecture and our plan is to take in as much as possible. We start with breakfast in the historical heart of the city at grand old dining establishment Sanborns Restaurant (see opposite). Drive by El Zócalo on the way, which is at its most beautiful in the early morning light, and stop to admire the great fusion of belle époque, art deco and neo-Aztec facades that surround it.

We've mixed in a healthy dose of contemporary culture in the middle of the day, with a trip to La Colección Jumex (see p034), the country's most exciting modern art collection, housed in a juice factory on the northern outskirts of the city, then it's back to the galleries of Roma, the centre of the contemporary art world, where Mexico's young, creative movers and shakers are to be found. You'll find some of the best boutiques here, too, and you can lunch at hip hangout Contramar (see p036). Finally, it's time to head down south, to the peaceful, leafy enclave of San Ángel, to check out Frida Kahlo and Diego Rivera's Houses and Studios (see p038). End the day in the best way possible, sipping a tequila cocktail in the courtyard of the San Ángel Inn (see p038).

For all addresses, see Resources.

10.00 Sanborns Restaurant

Sanborns is a chain of stores where you'll find everything you need, from magazines to aspirins and wedding cakes. The original branch is housed in Casa de los Azulejos, an old colonial building in the heart of the city centre, with a facade covered in blue tiles. At its centre is an airy restaurant (above) in a colonnaded, high-ceilinged, covered courtyard, which is flooded with light from above. Unpretentious Mexican food is served here, and the breakfasts, in particular, shouldn't be missed. Enjoy pint-sized fruit juices, *huevos rancheros* (tortilla topped with eggs and spicy sauce), *chilaquiles* (tortilla chips with salsa and grilled cheese) and *molletes* (Mexican pizza), while admiring the 1925 mural by José Clemente Orozco and watching the Mexican business breakfasts at work.
Francisco I Madero 4, T 5510 1331

11.30 La Colección Jumex

Located in a high-security bunker within the Jumex juice-factory complex is the biggest collection of international contemporary art in Latin America, with 1,200 pieces. The owner is Eugenio López, a major patron of contemporary art in the country, whose family founded Jumex. Open weekdays only, by appointment.
Km 19.5 Carretera México-Pachuca, T 5775 8188, www.lacoleccionjumex.org

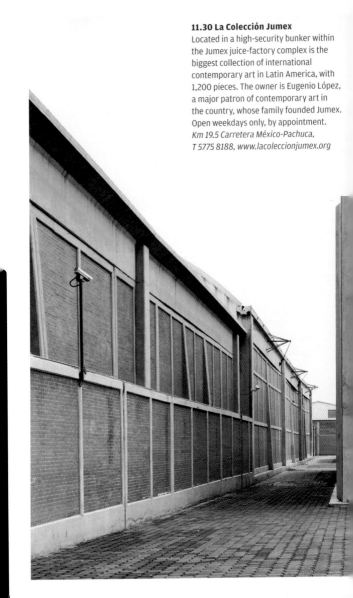

13.00 Contramar

This is *the* place to lunch in Mexico City these days. A seafood restaurant that launched more than five years ago, with another branch in Guadalajara (see p100), it is still one of the city's most fashionable eateries. Its success is down to a mix of fabulous food, simple and unpretentious decor, with a hint of old-school cantina about it and the eclectic mix of artists, fashionistas, businessmen and families who frequent it. Join them and enjoy the delights on offer, such as shrimp tacos, octopus tostadas, seared tuna and a cool *micheladas*: Pacifico beer on ice and lime, which is served in a salt-rimmed glass. *Durango 200, T 5514 9217*

14.30 Galería OMR

Contemporary art is booming here. What began with the rise of Gabriel Orozco in the early 1990s, has developed into an international phenomenon, which has spawned superstars, such as the ex-pat Mexican, Carlos Amorales, as well as the Belgian, Francis Alys, and the Spaniard, Santiago Sierra. The scene continues to grow, fed recently by the work of artists such as Miguel Calderón, Pedro Reyes and Stefan Bruggemann, nurtured by a close-knit network of galleries, including OMR, founded in 1983 by Jaime Riestra and Patricia Ortiz Monasterio. Located in an early-1900s house in a beautiful plaza, it shows the work of American Thomas Glassford (such as this light from his 'Aster' series, above) and Erick Beltrán. *Plaza Río de Janeiro 54, T 5207 1080, www.galeriaomr.com*

16.00 Frida Kahlo and Diego Rivera's Houses and Studios
These modernist masterpieces are worth a visit, even though you can't go inside. Designed by Juan O'Gorman in 1929, there are two separate structures (one red, one blue), joined by a bridge and enclosed by a dramatic cactus fence. Afterwards, head for the San Ángel Inn (T 5616 1402), for drinks and dinner.
Diego Rivera 2, T 5550 1518

URBAN LIFE

CAFÉS, RESTAURANTS, BARS AND NIGHTCLUBS

The return of inner-city urbanity is the definitive sign of Mexico City's new vitality. For decades it seemed condemned to US-style freeways, shopping malls and suburbanisation, but the recent regeneration of old live-and-work *colonias*, or neighbourhoods, in the heart of the city, with their wide pedestrian boulevards and parks, shady trees and sidewalk cafés, has revitalised the centre. Sophisticated restaurants such as Ixchel (see p044) and Contramar (see p036), along with the rediscovery of traditional eateries, such as La Opera (see p050), and the popularity of simple cantinas like Covadonga (see p043) have provided the substance behind the hype. Lifestyle magazines such as *Celeste* and *Files*, and city guides such as *DF* and *Chilango* are useful for keeping up to date.

Mexican nouvelle cuisine leans heavily on two ingredients: *flor de calabaza,* or courgette flowers, and *cuitlacoche*, a type of Mexican truffle (see p087). Tourists should be as ready to sample local food off the neighbourhood streets, such as *quesadillas*, *sopes* and *tostadas*, which are all variations on a filled tortilla theme, as to pile into a plate of tacos in a dining hotspot.

Nightlife starts here with late dinner in one of the city's reputed restaurants, such as Ligaya (Nuevo León 68, T 5286 6268), moving on to a bar in one of the cooler hotels, and ending up, after many tequilas, at a clandestine late-licence spot or private party.
For all addresses, see Resources.

The Blue Lounge

This is one of the more seductive corners of the reappointed Camino Real hotel (see p028). It's an airy oasis, with a timeless elegance that's perfectly in tune with Ricardo Legorreta's 1960s hotel building. The place lends itself to idle cocktail quaffing, and the great and the good are often to be found here doing just that. You'll lounge on blue-upholstered Harry Bertoia chairs, resting on a glass floor that is suspended over a pool strewn with pebbles (above). The evening crowds are often entertained by live music here. If you don't have rooms booked at Camino Real, then a visit to The Blue Lounge is the perfect excuse to have a nosey round the interior of Ricardo Legorreta's masterpiece.
Mariano Escobedo 700, T 5263 8888, www.caminoreal.com/mexico

The Terrace

After it opened in 2003, it didn't take long for this bar, located in the W Mexico City hotel (see p024), to become one of the starriest hangouts in the city. The generous space provides all the elements for an evening of elegant idling, with low-level seating, a cityscape backdrop and ambient lighting. There is also a private bar-within-a-bar, a space conceived in true modernist Mexican style, contained in a red concrete box suspended above the main deck (above). There may be a chance to shake a leg later in the evening, but be warned: girls, you can be sure that the legs around you will be longer, lankier and more tanned than yours; and guys, they will be better shod. After all, we're talking first-class loafing.
Campos Elíseos 252, T 9138 1800, www.starwoodhotels.com/whotels

Covadonga

This old cantina is proof that the cool crowd doesn't always require Philippe Starck-designed lights and arrangements of rare orchids to pull them in. Covadonga has been serving traditional Spanish food since the 1950s, and its no-nonsense furniture and fittings and double-height ceiling preserve the spirit of those days. In the evenings, old Spanish ex-pats play dominoes here, while artists gather regularly for drinks and food after going to exhibition openings in the neighbourhood.
Puebla 121, T 5533 2701

Ixchel

Located in an early-20th-century house, Ixchel restaurant and bar was one of the pioneers of Roma's renaissance, when it opened in 1994. It has been refurbished since then, but persists as a haunt of local artists and writers. The smart restaurant upstairs (above) serves mouthwatering dishes that demonstrate a successful Asian-Mediterranean fusion. Downstairs is a terrace bar, and a lounge bar done out in blue velvet. A classic evening of idling in Roma should definitely include a spell of drinking martinis here.
Medellin 65, T 5208 4055

El Nivel

Located between Templo Mayor (the ruins of the Aztec city) and El Zócalo, El Nivel, which opened in 1855, proudly boasts the first licence to sell alcohol in the country. Not that it flaunts this honour. Its interior (above), with its faded green walls crowded with wonky pictures, is wonderfully understated and seemingly frozen in time, somewhere around the middle of last century. It used to be the building where the water level (*el nivel*) in Mexico City was measured. Now, it's the perfect pit stop for liquid refreshments in the shape of cold Victoria beers, providing a welcome respite from the chaos of the heat, the crowds, the street vendors and, above all, the Aztec dancers outside.
Moneda 2, T 5522 9755

La Rambla Loncheria

This is probably not the usual guidebook fare. In fact, even to the locals, it's quite an ordinary establishment. But we love it for its pink and red interior and turkey tortas and tacos, which are the ideal cure for a tequila hangover. Like many other traditional businesses in El Centro, La Rambla Loncheria has made no effort to update in the past umpteen decades. It has just been waiting for its moment to arrive. And that moment is now, along with a tourism attuned to the charms of recent design history. Red leatherette banquettes on which to enjoy dribbly local fast food? Who could say no?
Motolinia 38, T 5512 9260

Restaurant DO

Polanco's Restaurant DO (its full name 'Denominación de Origen', is Spain's official stamp of authenticity for produce such as wine, cheese and ham) opened in December 2003. Emerging architecture group Higuera + Sánchez was brought in to dress the space, previously occupied by an Italian restaurant. It's now a series of bars, lounges and dining rooms, with a terrace, styled minimally but with the odd baroque touch. It pulls in the smart local set in search of a taste of Jamón de Ibérico de Bellota washed down with a temperanillo and live music. Chef Pablo San Roman cooks up contemporary Spanish cuisine, in the form of tapas and *pintxos,* as well as full dishes, and the cellar is full of classics from the Peninsula.
Calle Hegel 406, T 5255 0612,
www.denominaciondeorigendo.com

La Opera

Located in the heart of the city's historic centre, La Opera dates from the early 1900s. It has an opulent, baroque interior with red booths and elaborate gold flourishes in the decorations. But, despite this grandeur it has no pretensions, and is a busy, affordable spot in which to grab lunch or a tequila on a trawl around El Centro. Locals will point out the bullet hole in the ceiling, which was made by Mexican revolutionary hero, Pancho Villa, upon his arrival in the city after the revolution of 1910.
5 de Mayo 10, T 5512 8959

Terrasse Renault

Renault is promoting its zippy, urban runabout cars by creating a string of global 'brand spaces'. After opening an atelier in Paris, a museum in Buenos Aires and cafés in Rome and Bogotá, their sleek Terrasse Renault in Mexico City is the latest project. Entasis Architects built a versatile space, with a restaurant serving modern French cuisine, courtesy of chef, Olivier Lombard. They also installed

a solid granite bar (above), which is backed by wooden latticing through which visitors can glimpse the Renault Zone, where art shows and car prototypes are exhibited. *Avenida Presidente Masaryk 214, T 5281 3482, www.renault-terrasse.com.mx*

Tiki Bar
Essentially a Polynesian theme bar,
Tiki Bar is drawing a young, well-heeled
crowd. This is thanks to the credentials
of its British owners, Jaspar Eyears,
a mixologist who earned his colours at
prestigious London bars like the Met bar
(T 00 44 20 7447 1000) and Crispin
Somerville, internationally renowned DJ.
227 Querétaro, T 5584 2668,
www.tiki.com.mx

INSIDER'S GUIDE

ADRIANA LARA, ARTIST

Adriana Lara, together with Fernando Mesta, Agustina Ferreyra and Diego Berruecos, runs an art-production agency called Perros Negros (www.perrosnegros.info), which is currently working on an international quarterly magazine called *Pazmaker*. The agency has also produced 'The Book' by Los Super Elegantes, a celebrated local 'art band', and a catalogue of their last project.

Adriana lives and works in Mexico's city centre. The Perros Negros office is located at Francisco I Madero 35, and she moved into a converted flat in the Banco Mexicano Building on Motolinia Street when El Centro started its regeneration programme a few years ago. She's worried that the changes occurring in El Centro will mean that traditional businesses and lifestyles will be displaced, and so she's a fierce supporter of local businesses. Her favourite hangouts are the 24-hour Chinese and Mexican cafés in 5 de Mayo: Café el Popular (5 de Mayo 52, T 5518 6081), Jugos Canada (5 de Mayo 47), and vintage bookshops on Donceles. She buys vintage clothes from streetsellers and her favourite markets: Lagunilla (Rayon Héroe de Granaditas/Bolivar Allende) and Pino Suárez (Benito Juárez/Aquiles Serdán).

Under the stage name, Lasser Moderna, she sings with Emilio Acevedo, playing local venues, such as Pasagüero (Motolinia 33, T 5512 6624), Cultural Roots (Tacuba 81, T 1041 6848) and Dos Naciones (Bolívar 58, T 5526 5867), as well as venues abroad.

ARCHITOUR

A GUIDE TO MEXICO CITY'S ICONIC BUILDINGS

Despite the growing international reputations of local masters, such as TEN and Higuera & Sánchez Architects, what springs to mind when we think of 20th-century Mexican architecture is still the work of Luis Barragán. Examples of his colourful style, tagged 'emotional architecture', are scattered across the city. In one narrow, unprepossessing street lies Casa Barragán/Ortega (General Francisco Ramírez 20, T 5515 4908), built in the 1940s, which marked the end of his functionalist experiments and modestly anticipates his masterpiece, Casa Barragán (see p068), which he built seven years later, for his own use, further up the same street.

The much-photographed pink block of Casa Gilardi (General León 82, T 5515 4908), completed by an 80-year-old Barragán in 1976, offers an interesting contrast. And, for a glimpse of his non-residential projects, you should head north-west of the city towards Naucalpan and stop off at Torres de Satélite (see p012).

Ricardo Legorreta has carried the torch for colourful Mexican modernism into the present day. Camino Real (see p028), built in the 1970s, was his work, as is The Juárez Complex (see p064). For another take on colour, Juan O'Gorman's houses-cum-studios for Diego Rivera and Frida Kahlo (see p038) shouldn't be missed while a visit to Ciudad Universitaria (see opposite) will reveal the slant on Mexican modernism taken by Barragán's peers.

For all addresses, see Resources.

Ciudad Universitaria

Constructed between 1950 and 1952, on solidified lava fields to the south of the city, Ciudad Universitaria represented the climax of Mexican modernism. Designed by the top architects of the time, led by Mario Pani and Enrique del Moral, it not only pooled the architectural talents of a generation, but is an excellent example of the Mexican love of integrating art and architecture. Architect Juan O'Gorman was responsible for the imposing library building (above), which carries striking pre-Hispanic motifs and designs, which explore historical and cultural themes. La Rectoria is adorned with murals by David Alfaro Siqueiros, one of the pillars of the 20th-century muralist movement. His 3D artwork on the side of La Rectoria (overleaf) has revolutionary overtones.
Avenida Insurgentes Sur, Pedregal

La Rectoria, Ciudad Universitaria

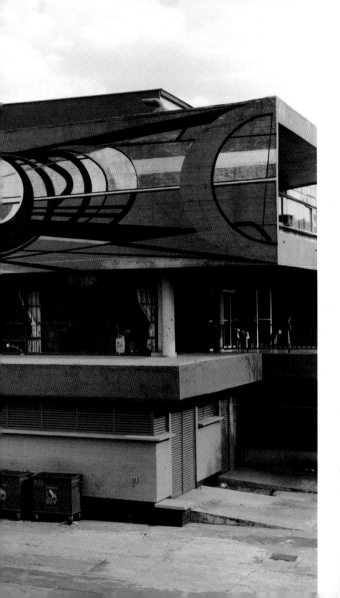

Torre Latinoamericana

Designed by Augusto H Álvarez in the 1950s, this was the city's first skyscraper, reaching to 182m and, for a while, it was the tallest building in Latin America. It is a symbol of the beginning of Mexico City's modern era and still stands, a distinctive modernist monument among the colonial buildings in the centre. It has survived violent earthquakes and considerable neglect towards the end of the century.

Bought by Carlos Slim's Carso Group, it is now being spruced up as part of the city-centre regeneration. If you get the chance, take the lift (above), which still has a lift attendant, and go to the viewing platform and café up on the top three floors, for spectacular 360-degree views of the city. *Francisco I Madero/Eje Central Lázaro Cárdenas, T 5518 7423, www.torrelatino.com*

Palacio Postal

This belle-époque bastion was built in
1907 by Italian architect Adamo Boari,
who later designed the exterior of the
Museo del Palacio de Bellas Artes (T 5512
1410) next door, during the regime of
Porfirio Díaz, a soldier and politician, who
became Mexico's president in 1876 and
remained in power until 1911. The glow
from the gilded interior of the building
hits you from the street. It's as if a gold
paintball has exploded inside and touched
every surface. Amazingly, this ornate
space still functions as a post office. So,
to give yourself an excuse to go in, buy
some old postcards from the streetsellers
outside and go and buy some stamps.
While you wait to be served, you can
check the place out at close quarters and
experience the rare treat of drumming
your fingers on gold and marble counters.
Tacuba 1/Eje Central Lázaro Cárdenas,
T 5512 0091

The Juárez Complex
In a huge area located alongside
Alameda Central park, which had been
largely abandoned since the 1985
earthquake, Ricardo Legorreta has
designed a public space, comprising
plazas and arcades, office towers,
government offices and housing.
The site is breathing new life into
the city centre. *Avenida Juárez*

Espacio Escultórico

Located in the Ciudad Universitaria area, Espacio Escultórico is a gigantic sculpture space, which was created in 1979 by a group of artists, headed by Mathias Goeritz. Their intention was to sculpt a large public space in which distinctions between sculpture and architecture, spectator and experience, could be erased. Created in a dramatic volcanic landscape, it consists of a huge, natural solidified lava bed, measuring 120m in diameter, encircled by a wall carved out of the volcanic rock. Surrounding the crater are 64 identical, evenly spaced, geometric, concrete sculptures (above). *Ciudad Universitaria, Avenida Insurgentes Sur, Pedregal*

Casa Barragán

Built in 1947, by modernist master, Luis Barragán, for his own use, this house represents his synthesis of the modern and traditional, resulting in a timeless, independent style. It was his home until he died, and everything in it has been left as it was when he was alive: books crammed onto a wall of shelves, a wastepaper bin hovering in the hallway, his dusty car still in the garage. The rooms are full of light and colour and the garden, which was sculpted by Barragán himself, is a beautiful, semi-organised wilderness. Visits are by appointment only. The Casa Museo organises trips here and also to view other Barragán works, such as nearby Casa Barragán/Ortega and Casa Gilardi (call the number below to book). *General Francisco Ramírez 14, T 5515 4908, www.barragan-foundation.com*

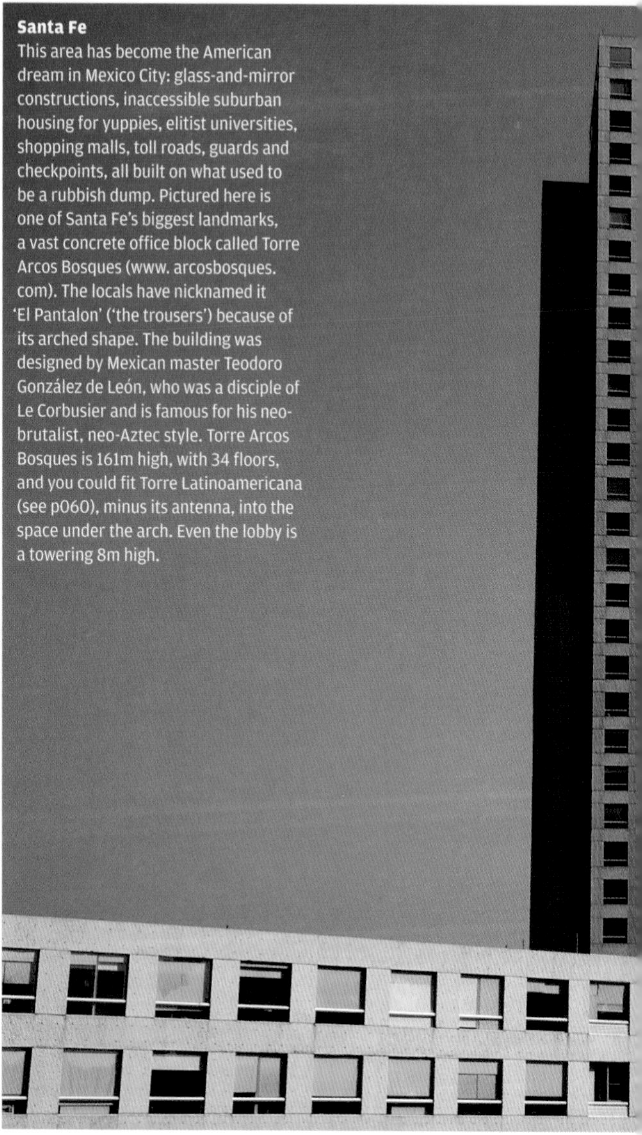

Santa Fe

This area has become the American dream in Mexico City: glass-and-mirror constructions, inaccessible suburban housing for yuppies, elitist universities, shopping malls, toll roads, guards and checkpoints, all built on what used to be a rubbish dump. Pictured here is one of Santa Fe's biggest landmarks, a vast concrete office block called Torre Arcos Bosques (www. arcosbosques. com). The locals have nicknamed it 'El Pantalon' ('the trousers') because of its arched shape. The building was designed by Mexican master Teodoro González de León, who was a disciple of Le Corbusier and is famous for his neo-brutalist, neo-Aztec style. Torre Arcos Bosques is 161m high, with 34 floors, and you could fit Torre Latinoamericana (see p060), minus its antenna, into the space under the arch. Even the lobby is a towering 8m high.

SHOPPING

THE CITY'S BEST SHOPS AND WHAT TO BUY

Neglected for decades by all but sight-seeking tourists, El Centro offers up stores that have remained gloriously unchanged for more than 50 years, and that includes the stock. Boots look as if they've walked back to the shelves from the Beatles era, and hat shops sell a great line in old-fashioned homburgs. A shopping spree in Centro and Alameda can throw up fantastic retro pieces. The markets, which are scattered throughout the city, yield crafts from all over the country, such as Yucatán hammocks, plant pots for pennies and *rebozos* (traditional scarves worn over the head and shoulders). Our favourite markets are Ciudadela (Balderas/Emilio Donde) and Coyoacán (Allende/Xicoténactl). At Fonart (Avenida Juárez 89, T 5521 0171), a shop run by a government agency promoting local crafts, you can also buy indigenous souvenirs. The prices are high, but the quality is guaranteed.

Polanco provides Rodeo-Drive-style shopping, if you're looking for international design and the Mexican equivalent. Shops such as Tane (Avenida Presidente Masaryk 430, T 5282 6200), which sells upscale silverware, are worth a visit. But the hip boutiques are in Condesa and Roma, where you'll find the best contemporary art galleries, design stores and independent fashion stores. Mexico has a distinctive design aesthetic, which transcends the eras and is very collectable; contemporary Mexican art is also hot property. *For all addresses, see Resources.*

Galería Méxicana de Diseño

This must-visit furniture and industrial-design store has, for the past 10 years, specialised in contemporary pieces by international and Mexican designers. If you make room in your packing for just one large item, we recommend that it's the 'Acapulco' chair (above), MXN1,600. Made from weatherproof materials, this is a surprisingly solid construction, fashioned in the iconic style of the eponymous beach resort, which recalls elegant loafing on sun-soaked terraces by the likes of Liz Taylor during the 1950s, the town's golden era. Available in a variety of colours including red, white, blue and, the one that jumped into our luggage and onto the terrace back home, turquoise (shown here).

Anatole France 13, T 5280 0080,
www.galeriamexicana.net

Poltrona Visual

The architect Bernardo Gómez-Pimienta has designed and furnished a number of key contemporary establishments in the city, such as super-minimal hotel, Habita (see p026). During a stay here, it's hard not to fall for his ceramics, which are used at breakfast time. These chunky pieces, such as this espresso cup and saucer, MXN100 and jug, MXN280 (below), are unmistakably modern in design, while adhering to the solid, graphic aesthetics of vintage Mexico. Poltrona Visual is dedicated to Bernardo's designs, which include great lights and furniture, too. It's on a busy main artery in San Ángel, so you could drop in on the way to see Frida Kahlo and Diego Rivera's houses (see p038).
Avenida Revolución 1566, T 5661 8889

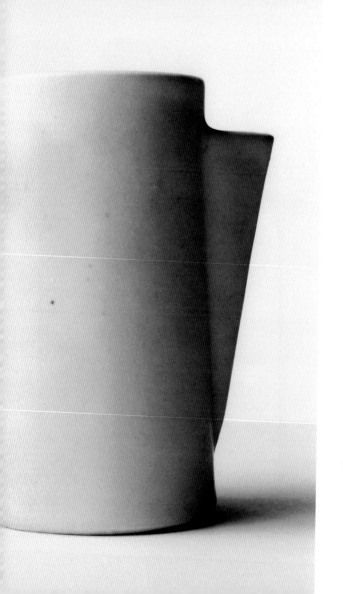

Chic by Accident

The charismatic collector, French-born Emmanuel Picault, is behind this fabulous haul of 20th-century design, examples of which are shown (above), prices on application. Some are iconic designs from around the world, but many are one-offs, sourced in Mexico, his adopted homeland: these travel candlesticks (left), MXN8,025, are a Mexican design from the 1970s. If restoration is necessary, he'll undertake it himself. The store and workshop ramble over several floors, and the place is a magnet, especially in the late afternoon, for members of the area's close-knit art-and-design community, who are often to be found lounging decorously in the collection of chairs, cigarette in hand, flicking ash into Murano-glass ashtrays. *Colima 180, T 5514 5723, www.chicbyaccident.com*

Sanborns

The Mexican beauty industry is something of a wasteland, which is surprising, given the amount of attention to detail that is bestowed on appearances and grooming, especially by the men. But, among the mountains of over-familiar imports to be found in Mexico City stores, Mexican shopping institution and department store chain Sanborns has this gem: an old-fashioned, rose-scented moisturising cream (above), called Crema Teatrical, MXN35. It won't erase wrinkles, rejuvenate jowls or banish blemishes, and will take your beauty regime right back to basics, but it will look stylishly retro in your bathroom cabinet, and lasts an eternity.
Casa de los Azulejos, Francisco I Madero 4, T 5512 1331

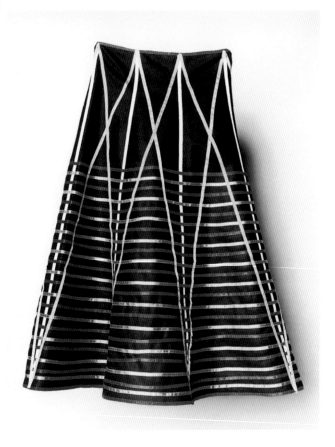

Local

This boutique features the work of young, contemporary fashion designers from the city. Many of them give their creations touches of traditional Mexican handiwork, from handwoven fabric, to trimmings made by indigenous women, or designs inspired by traditional crafts. A little searching produces some unique and desirable pieces and recent collections have featured some unusual souvenirs (literally), such as a simple shift dress with a hand-embroidered image of the Torre Latinoamericana (see p060). We would recommend the work of Carla Fernandez, who is particularly adept at blending her contemporary designs with local crafts, as seen in this Falda Amuzga skirt (above), from MXN2,000, which makes a feature of traditional hand-woven ribbons.
Amsterdam 248, T 5564 9148

Tardan

Days can be lost in this brilliant fossil of the 1950s, despite it's central position in the tourist hub of the city. It looks as if it might have only just opened its doors and dusted off its stock after an interval lasting half a century. Skip over the great profusion of sombreros (a tourist trap that's probably responsible for keeping the store's doors open). We love it for its timeless trilbies and homburgs (above), from MXN2,160 each, beautifully made, with old-fashioned precision and finish. Charm the staff and you might get a free feather in your cap...
Plaza de la Constitución 7, T 5512 3902, www.tardan.com.mx

Casa de Guayaberas Carr

Worn by statesmen and bridegrooms in Mexico for decades, a 'Guayabera' shirt (above), MXN900, is the epitome of style when it's teamed with a nice pair of slacks (and the authentic versions, from the Guayabera region of Mexico, don't come cheap). There are many variations on the theme, including embroidered panels, elaborate tucking detail, long or short sleeves, and plenty of colours to choose from. Pick a simple style, in a tame colour, and it won't look amiss if you combine it with shorts and Havaianas (flip-flops) for stylish poolside posturing.
López 13, T 5521 2729

Herramientes del Siglio XXI

As well as the vintage-seekers' paradise, Chic by Accident (see p076), Emmanuel Picault has also set up a satellite business, Herramientes del Siglio XXI (Tools of the 21st Century). From his workshop behind the Chic by Accident store, he produces beautiful, hand-fashioned pieces, made to order, which have been inspired by classic Mexican design. This mahogany chaise longue (above), which costs MXN22,927, is a good example of his work. It has the heavy primitive curves of traditional pieces of furniture, but these have been streamlined and upholstered to suit 21st-century tastes.

Colima 180, T 5514 5723

Herradura Blanco Tequila

There's a lot of wool pulled over the eyes of tequila tourists and often bottles that look the part promise more than they deliver. The best are the 100 per cent agave tequilas, because, unlike the blended varieties, these premium tequilas are distilled from the Weber blue agave, a plant that's native to Mexico. Production is closely scrutinised by the government to ensure that exacting standards are maintained. Silver, or blanco, tequila, such as the Herradura Blanco Tequila (above), MXN269, is bottled direct, offering an explosion of flavour, which is unmellowed by wooden casks. Available from La Europea (T 5661 5160) and other supermarkets, it offers a fair taste at a fair price. It also bears the stamp that guarantees it's 100 per cent agave and 100 per cent Guadalajara produce.

Iker Ortiz

It's easy to get sucked into frittering away your pesos on market tat, especially if it's homespun jewellery. Instead, our advice is to sidestep the ethnic offerings and seek out the work of Iker Ortiz. This third-generation jeweller's designs are simple and straight-talking and, as a result, they are strong players on the international design scene. You can buy his work from the Museo Tamayo Arte Contemporáneo shop (T 5286 6519). We loved the bowed triangularity and cool understatement of his Corian rings (above), MXN200 each, also available in steel. Visitors to his workshop, located in the centre of the city, can order individually made pieces. *Miguel Angel de Quevado 140, T 5663 2924, www.i-ka.com*

La Primavera Vidrio Soplado

A tour around Casa Barragán (see p068) is guaranteed to open your eyes to the world of decorative mirrored balls. Even aficionados of Luis Barragán's work might not have clocked his love of spheres, but the interior of his house is littered with sculptural mirrored balls, from bowling ball to Spacehopper proportions. La Primavera Vidrio Soplado, a glassware outlet that used to be housed in a chaotic, unannounced space in a Roma back street, has recently set up a more organised retail space nearby. It still hawks a higgledy piggledy mixture of glass basics and curiosities, including mirrored-glass spheres such as this (above), approx MXN150, to help you recreate Barragán chic back home.
Colima 264, T 5207 1159,
www.laprimaveravidriosoplado.com.mx

Contemporary Local Cuisine

It may seem a bit perverse, picking up tins of vegetables in a country known for its wealth of tasty, fresh food, but we revelled in the breadth of canned consumables available in the supermarkets (the chilli selection alone takes up a whole aisle). These are the favourite ingredients of contemporary local cuisine (above), so they were our chosen souvenirs: *flor de calabaza* (courgette flowers), MXN15.50 each and *cuitlacoche* (a type of Mexican truffle with a smoky flavour), MXN19.50 each. Pick them up at most supermarkets and use them to put a modern Mexican stamp on omelettes back at home.

SPORTS AND SPAS

WORK OUT, CHILL OUT OR JUST WATCH

International competition has given Mexico some of its greatest sporting landmarks. Estadio Olímpico Universitario (see p092) was built for the 1968 Olympics, as was Estadio Azteca (Calzada Tlalpan 3465, T 5617 8080), which went on to be used for the 1970 and 1986 Football World Cups. Naturally, football fanaticism dominates the sports fields, with América, Cruz Azul and Pumas being the biggest teams (for information, visit www.futmex.com). Bullfighting also commands a following and the city flaunts the biggest bullring in the world: Plaza México in Noche Buena (Augusto Rodin 241, T 5563 3959), which has 48,000 seats. More quirky spectator sports include a form of Basque favourite *pelota* (a game played in a court with a ball and a wickerwork raquet) and also wrestling, although their popularity is waning.

When it comes to keeping fit, those not refining their physique at Condesa's Qi Gym (see opposite) may be found pounding the parks, especially those in Condesa and Chapultepec. Visitors are welcome to join them and can merge their morning fitness regimes with a spot of sightseeing. Spa culture is seeping into upscale urban life here. The better hotels, such as Habita (see p026), offer simple, stylish facilities and treatments, but Away Spa (see p094), at W Mexico City (see p024), brings a sense of place to proceedings with a *temazcal* (ancient steam bath) among its five-star fittings. *For all addresses, see Resources.*

Qi Gym

Situated in the fashionable Condesa area, this is where the young and beautiful go to work out. The gym is a contemporary construction, designed by Higuera & Sánchez Architects, and it houses four floors of the most up-to-the-minute equipment. As well as the gym, there's a spa, wall-climbing facilities (above) and a yoga studio. This is, without doubt, the most stylish place in the city to hit the treadmills, but it's also a good place to go if you just want to chill out with a fresh fruit juice, a steam and a massage. Your hotel should be able to arrange day membership for you. There's a very good sports-and-wellbeing boutique on the ground floor, where you can pick up some treats to spoil yourself with back at home. *Ámsterdam 317, T 5574 5095, www.qi.com.mx*

Reception Area, Qi Gym

Estadio Olímpico Universitario

Built in 1952, this 73,000-capacity stadium is both a sporting and an architectural landmark. It took centre stage during the 1968 Olympics, hosting the opening and closing ceremonies, as well as all the field and track events in between. Today, it is the home ground of Pumas, one of Mexico City's biggest football teams. Located in Ciudad Universitaria (see p057), built on a former lava field, it was designed to look like a volcanic crater by architect Augusto Pérez Palacios. Rather than build upwards, using concrete and steel, he dug out the stepped terraces from the volcanic rock, using the rocks he extracted to construct the exterior walls. The decoration of these walls was handed over to Diego Rivera, who used rocks to create the murals. *Ciudad Universitaria, Avenida Insurgentes Sur, Pedregal*

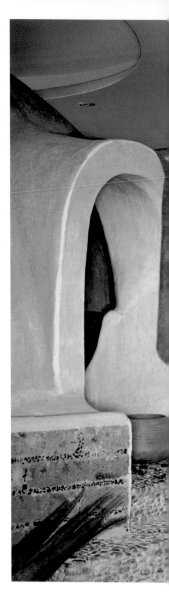

Away Spa

This spa, which is located in W Mexico City hotel (see p024), has gone for a mix of old and new in its rejuvenating offerings. Interrupting the sleek design of the pool, treatment rooms and relaxation area is a *temazcal* (right), which is a traditional wattle-and-daub domed steam room. The indigenous population has used steam baths like these to cure all ills for centuries. They believe that combining the properties of fire and water purifies mind, body and soul, and rids you of, among other things, any tensions and worries. You can follow a session in the steam bath here with a massage, for good measure, be it aromatherapy, shiatsu, Swedish or deep-tissue. There are myriad facial treatments to choose from, and various body wraps too, as well as a well-equipped fitness area.
Campos Elíseos 252, T 9138 1800, www.starwoodhotels.com/whotels

ESCAPES

WHERE TO GO IF YOU WANT TO LEAVE TOWN

When it often takes a couple of hours just to cross the city by car, it's little surprise that getting out of town requires much effort and good traffic nerves. It's worth it, though, to see some of the country's famous historical sites, such as the pre-Hispanic pyramids of the ancient city of Teotihuacán (see opposite) and the statues and pyramids of Tula, which are located within 100km of the city to the north. Leave early to beat the traffic and the crowds (both are big tourist sites) and make an appointment to visit La Colección Jumex (see p034), for a good modern art pose mid route.

To the south and west, around Cuernavaca, you will find the out-of-town retreats of the city's more privileged inhabitants peppering the hillsides. If no personal invitation is in the offing, head to Tepoztlán, an attractive town in the hills, with craft shops and restaurants, and Taxco, with its cobbled streets, dominated by the silver-mining industry (there are jewellery shops aplenty). Or visit Malinalco, with its Aztec ruins, set in beautiful surroundings.

Those who hunger for large dollops of urban buzz and contemporary culture, can supplement Mexico City's offerings with a trip to the country's second city, Guadalajara (see p100). Also, within two hours you can be at either of Mexico's hot, sandy coasts: Acapulco (see p098), to the west, a retreat of the rich and famous since 1950; or east, to sub-tropical Veracruz (see p102).

For all addresses, see Resources.

Teotihuacán

The most spectacular of the pre-Hispanic cities, which had already been abandoned by the time the Spaniards arrived. Take a walk up Calzada de los Muertos (Street of the Dead) and you can see why this was known as the city where men transformed themselves into gods. At one end of the street is the Pyramid of the Moon, at the other end is the Temple of Quezalcóatl (above), covered with stone carvings of plumed serpents, and to one side stands the Pyramid of the Sun. Before you go, sample the delights of Restaurant La Gruta (T 59 4956 0127), a grotto full of coloured chairs on the outskirts. Try the *quesadillas* (folded tortillas), *chicharrón* (a traditional meat dish) and *pozole* (soup or stew). Or you could stay the night at nearby Villas Arqueológicas (T 55 5836 9020).

East of Mexico City on highway to Pachuca

Las Brisas

Mexico City locals escape to Acapulco at
weekends, to play on its beaches. In the
1950s, it was a glamorous destination
for the world's elite. Recapture this old-
style glamour at Las Brisas (pictured),
a pink 1950s hotel, with pink jeeps, plus
a beach club with an ocean swimming
pool, which even has pink rocks.
*Carretera Escénica 5255, Acapulco,
T 74 4469 6900, www.brisas.com.mx*

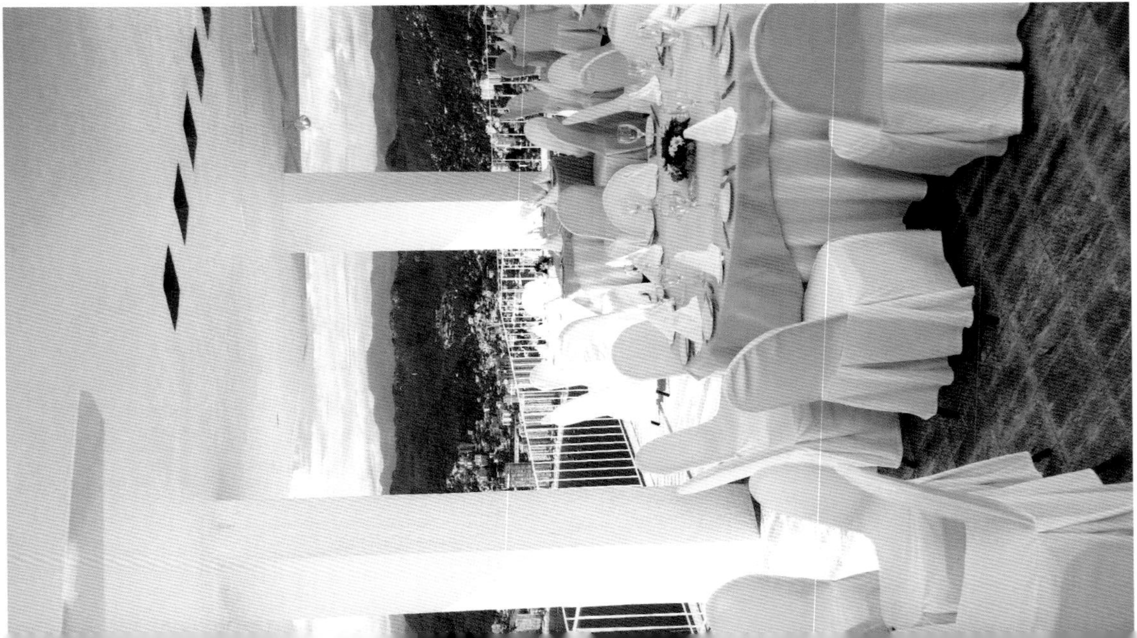

Guadalajara

Mexico's second city is famous as the home of mariachi bands and tequila, but it also has its own strong cultural identity. It is to Mexico City what Basel is to Berne and Barcelona is to Madrid. Locals say it's not a city, but a state of mind. 'The fact that nothing happens in Guadalajara is exactly what makes things happen,' says art promoter, Gabriela López Rochas, who helped to cultivate a contemporary art scene here by founding the OPA art centre (T 33 3613 6812), at the top of modernist jewel, Condominio Guadalajara. Striking buildings are everywhere, such as the Light of the World Church (above) and the Santa Rita Church (left). As the birthplace of Luis Barragán, the city has a rich 20th-century architectural heritage and the Tlaquepaque area has become a centre for ceramic design and handicrafts.

Azúcar

Hotelier Carlos Couturier has the design-Mexico City hotel scene sewn up, with Habita (see p026) and Condesa DF (see p020), as well as Hotel Básico (T 98 4879 4448) in Playa del Carmen. The latest addition to his empire is Azúcar, which is a sophisticated retreat in the Gulf of Mexico. It's near the tiny town of San Rafael, with its pre-Hispanic Tajín ruins, and a mere 45-minute flight in a four-seater Cesna from the capital. There are 20 thatched bungalows (right), each with its own terrace and hammock. The atmosphere is intimate, but distinctly casual. An in-house restaurant serves simple, fresh fish, shrimp and oyster cocktails and grilled *acamayas* (freshwater langoustines). There's also a pool and spa to complete the perfect beach experience.

Azúcar, Km 83.5 Carretera Federal Nautla-Poza Rica, Veracruz, T 23 2321 0678, www.hotelazucar.com

NOTES
SKETCHES AND MEMOS

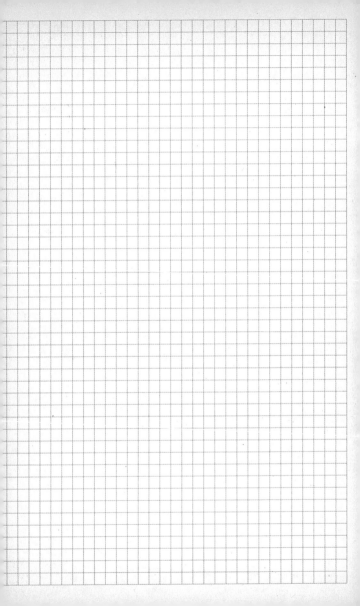

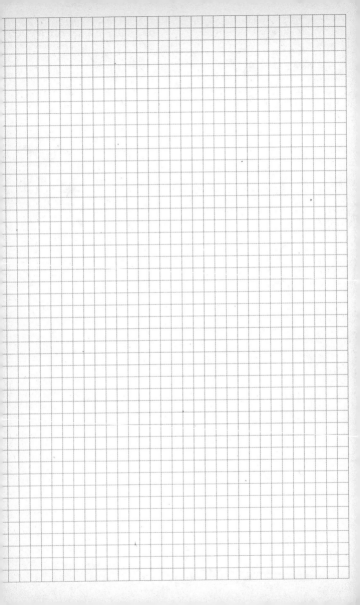

RESOURCES
ADDRESSES AND ROOM RATES

LANDMARKS

009 Catédral Metropolitana
El Zócalo

009 El Ángel de la Independencia
Paseo de la Reforma/ Rio Tiber

009 Palacio Nacional
Avenida Pino Suarez

011 Agustín Hernández's Home/Office
Bosque Acacias
T 5596 1554

012 Torres de Satélite
Periférico Norte
Ciudad Satélite

013 Basílica de Guadalupe
Plaza de las Américas 1
Villa de Guadalupe

014 Museo Nacional de Antropología
Paseo de la Reforma
T 5553 6253
www.mna.inah.gob.mx

HOTELS

016 Majestic
Room rates:
double, MXN1,300
Francisco I Madero 73
T 5521 8600

017 Gran Hotel
Room rates:
double, MXN2,160
Avenida 16 de Septiembre 82
T 1083 7700
www.granhotelciudad demexico.com.mx

020 Condesa DF
Room rates:
double, MXN2,230;
Balcony Suite, MXN2,800;
Top Suite, MXN4,450
Avenida Veracruz 102
T 5241 2600
www.condesadf.com

024 W Mexico City
Room rates:
double, MXN2,500;
Presidential Suite, MXN34,400;
Cool Corner Suite, MXN4,880
Campos Elíseos 252
T 9138 1800
www.starwood hotels.com/whotels

026 Habita
Room rates:
double, MXN3,040
Avenida Presidente Masaryk 201
T 5282 3100
www.hotelhabita.com

028 Camino Real
Room rates:
double, MXN2,000;
Presidential Suite, MXN28,700
Mariano Escobedo 700
T 5263 8888
www.caminoreal. com/mexico

030 Intercontinental Presidente
Room rates:
double, MXN2,700
Campos Elíseos 218
T 5327 7700
www.ichotelsgroup.com

24 HOURS

033 Sanborns Restaurant
Casa de los Azulejos
Francisco I Madero 4
T 5510 1331

034 La Colección Jumex
Km 19.5 Carretera México-Pachuca
T 5775 8188
www.lacoleccionjumex.org

036 Contramar
Durango 200
T 5514 9217

037 Galería OMR
Plaza Río de Janeiro 54
T 5207 1080
www.galeriaomr.com

038 Frida Kahlo and Diego Rivera's Houses and Studios
Diego Rivera 2
T 5550 1518

038 San Ángel Inn
Diego Rivera 50
Coyoacán
T 5616 1402
www.sanangelinn.com

URBAN LIFE

040 Ligaya
Nuevo León 68
T 5286 6268

041 The Blue Lounge
Mariano Escobedo 700
T 5263 8888
www.caminoreal.
com/mexico

042 The Terrace
W Mexico City
Campos Elíseos 252
T 9138 1800
www.starwood
hotels.com/whotels

043 Covadonga
Puebla 121
T 5533 2701

044 Ixchel
Medellin 65
T 5208 4055

046 El Nivel
Moneda 2
T 5522 9755

047 La Rambla Loncheria
Motolinia 38
T 5512 9260

048 Restaurant DO
Calle Hegel 406
T 5255 0612
www.denominacion
deorigendo.com

050 La Opera
5 de Mayo 10
T 5512 8959

051 Terrasse Renault
Avenida Presidente
Masaryk 214
T 5281 3482
www.renault-
terrasse.com.mx

052 Tiki Bar
Querétaro 227
T 5584 2668
www.tiki.com.mx

052 Met Bar
Metropolitan Hotel
19 Old Park Road
London
United Kingdom
T 00 44 20 7447 1000
www.metropolitan.como.bz

054 Café el Popular
5 de Mayo 52
T 5518 6081

054 Cultural Roots
Tacuba 81
T 1041 6848

054 Dos Naciones
Bolívar 58
T 5526 5867

054 Jugos Canada
5 de Mayo 47

054 Lagunilla
Rayon Héroe de
Granaditas/Bolivar Allende

054 Pasagüero
Motolinia 33
T 5512 6624

054 Pino Suárez
Benito Juárez/
Aquiles Serdán

ARCHITOUR

056 Casa Barragán/
Ortega
General Francisco
Ramírez 20
T 5515 4908
www.barragan-
foundation.com

056 Casa Gilardi
General León 82
T 5515 4908
www.barragan-
foundation.com

057 Ciudad
Universitaria
Avenida Insurgentes Sur
Pedregal

060 Torre
Latinoamericana
Francisco I Madero/Eje
Central Lázaro Cárdenas
T 5518 7423
www.torrelatino.com

062 Palacio Postal
Tacuba 1/Eje Central Lázaro
Cárdenas
T 5512 0091

062 Museo del Palacio
de Bellas Artes
Avenida Juárez/Eje Central
Lázaro Cárdenas
T 5512 1410
www.museobellasartes.com

064 The Juárez Complex
Avenida Juárez
066 Espacio Escultórico
Ciudad Universitaria
Avenida Insurgentes Sur
Pedregal
068 Casa Barragán
General Francisco
Ramírez 14
T 5515 4908
www.barragan-
foundation.com
070 Torre Arcos Bosques
Paseo de los
Tamarindos 400a
Bosques de las Lomas
www.arcosbosques.com

SHOPPING
072 Ciudadela Market
Balderas/Emilio Donde
072 Coyoacán Market
Allende/Xicoténactl
072 Fonart
Avenida Juárez 89
T 5521 0171
072 Tane
Avenida Presidente
Masaryk 430
T 5282 6200
073 Galería Méxicana
de Diseño
Anatole France 13
T 5280 0080
www.galeriamexicana.net

074 Poltrona Visual
Avenida Revolución 1566
T 5661 8889
076 Chic by Accident
Colima 180
T 5514 5723
www.chicbyaccident.com
078 Sanborns
Casa de Los Azulejos
Francisco I Madero 4
T 5512 1331
079 Local
Ámsterdam 248
T 5564 9148
080 Tardan
Plaza de la Constitución 7
T 5512 3902
www.tardan.com.mx
081 Casa de
Guayaberas Carr
López 13
T 5521 2729
082 Herramientas
del Siglo XXI
Colima 180
T 5514 5723
084 La Europa
Plaza 17 de Julio 6
T 5661 5160
085 Iker Ortiz
Miguel Angel de
Quevado 140
T 5663 2924
www.i-ka.com
085 Museo Tamayo
Arte Contemporáneo
Paseo de la Reforma/Gandhi
T 5286 6519
www.museotamayo.org

086 La Primavera
Vidrio Soplado
Colima 264
T 5207 1159
www.laprimaveravidrio
soplado.com.mx

SPORTS AND SPAS
088 Estadio Azteca
Calzada Tlalpan 3465
T 5617 8080
www.esmas.com/
estadioazteca
088 Plaza México
Augusto Rodin 241
Noche Buena
T 5563 3959
www.lamexico.com
089 Qi Gym
Ámsterdam 317
T 5574 5095
www.qi.com.mx
092 Estadio Olímpico
Universitario
Ciudad Universitaria
Avenida Insurgentes Sur
Pedregal
094 Away Spa
W Mexico City
Campos Elíseos 252
T 9138 1800
www.starwood
hotels.com/whotels

ESCAPES

097 Restaurant
La Gruta
Zona Arqueológica
Teotihuacán
T 59 4956 0127

097 Villas
Arqueológicas
Zona Arqueológica
Teotihuacán
T 55 5836 9020
www.teotihuacaninfo.com

098 Las Brisas
Carretera Escénica 5255
Acapulco
T 74 4469 6900
www.brisas.com.mx

100 OPA
Avenida 16 de
Septiembre 730
Guadalajara
T 33 3613 6812
www.opa.com.mx

102 Azúcar
Km 83.5 Carretera Federal
Nautla-Poza Rica
Veracruz
T 23 2321 0678
www.hotelazucar.com

102 Hotel Básico
Playa del Carmen
Quintana Roo
T 98 4879 4448
www.hotelbasico.com

WALLPAPER* CITY GUIDES

Editorial Director
Richard Cook

Art Director
Loran Stosskopf
City Editor
Pablo Léon de la Barra
Associate Writer
Emma Moore
Project Editor
Rachael Moloney
Series Editor
Jeroen Bergmans
**Executive
Managing Editor**
Jessica Firmin

Chief Designer
Ben Blossom
Designers
Sara Martin
Ingvild Sandal
Map Illustrator
Russell Bell

Photography Editor
Christopher Lands
Photography Assistant
Jasmine Labeau

Chief Sub-Editor
Lizzie Stoodley
Sub-Editor
Clive Morris

Editorial Assistants
Felicity Cloake
Milly Nolan
Olivia Salazar-Winspear

**Wallpaper* Group
Editor-in-Chief**
Jeremy Langmead
Creative Director
Tony Chambers
Publishing Director
Fiona Dent

Thanks to
Paul Barnes
Evgeniy Kazannik
David McKendrick
Meirion Pritchard
James Reid

PHAIDON

Phaidon Press Limited
Regent's Wharf
All Saints Street
London N1 9PA

Phaidon Press Inc
180 Varick Street
New York, NY 10014
www.phaidon.com

First published 2006
© 2006 Phaidon
Press Limited

ISBN 0 7148 4690 2

A CIP Catalogue record
for this book is available
from the British Library.

All prices are correct at
time of going to press,
but are subject to change.

Printed in China

PHOTOGRAPHERS

Henning Bock
Chic by Accident, p077

Dante Busquets
Basílica de Guadalupe, p013
Museo Nacional de Antropología, pp014-015
Gran Hotel, pp017-019
Camino Real, pp028-029
Frida Kahlo and Diego Rivera's Houses and Studios, pp038-039
Ixchel, pp044-045
La Opera, p050
Terrasse Renault, p051
Tiki Bar, pp052-053
Santa Fe, pp058-059
The Juárez Complex, pp064-065
Espacio Escultórico, pp066-067
Torre Arcos Bosques, pp070-071
Qi Gym, p89, pp090-091
Estadio Olimpíco Universitario, pp092-093

Douglas Friedman
Mexico City, City View, inside front cover
Augustín Hernández's Home/Office, pp010-011
Torres de Satélite, p012
W Mexico City, pp024-025

Sanborns Restaurant, p033
La Colección Jumex, pp034-035
Contramar, p036
Galería OMR, p037
The Blue Lounge, p041
The Terrace, p042
Covadonga, p043
El Nivel, p046
La Rambla Loncheria, p047
Adriana Lara, p055
Ciudad Universitaria, p057, pp058-059
Torre Latinoamericana, pp060-061
Palacio Postal, pp062-063
Casa Barragán, pp068-069
Galería Méxicana de Diseño, p073
Poltrona Visual, pp074-075
Chic by Accident, pp076-077
Sanborns, p078
Local, p079
Tardan, p080
Casa de Guayaberas Carr, p081
Herramientes del Siglio XXI, pp082-083
Herradura Blanco Tequila, p084
La Primavera Vidrio Soplado, p086
Contemporary Local Cuisine, p087
Away Spa, pp094-095
Guadalajara, pp100-101

Jaime Navarro
Condesa DF, pp020-021, pp022-023

Undine Pröhl
Azúcar, pp102-103

MEXICO CITY

A COLOUR-CODED GUIDE TO THE CITY'S HOT 'HOODS

CONDESA
The fashionable quarter: chic bars, tree-lined avenues and stylish new-builds

EL CENTRO
The city's historic heart, site of the old Aztec capital, is an exciting mix of old and new

ROMA
This is where the creative people gather, with the best galleries, shops and cafés

POLANCO
Upper East Side meets Beverly Hills in expensive restaurants, hotels and boutiques

ALAMEDA
An important part of the city centre, housing the most important landmarks

CHAPULTEPEC
This neighbourhood is one big park, a green and leafy interlude in the hustle and bustle

For a full description of each neighbourhood,
including the places you really must not miss, see the Introduction